G000255148

STATIONS OF THE CROSS

First published in 2001 by
THE COLUMBA PRESS
55A Spruce Avenue, Stillorgan Industrial Park,
Blackrock, Co Dublin

ISBN 1 85607 316 5

Designed by Bill Bolger
Printed in Ireland by Colour Books Ltd, Dublin

Copyright © 2001, The Parish of Firhouse

THE PARISH OF FIRHOUSE
CHURCH OF OUR LADY OF MOUNT CARMEL

STATIONS OF THE CROSS
by IMOGEN STUART

WITH A TEXT BY DESMOND FORRISTAL
PHOTOGRAPHS BY PETE SMYTH

the columba press

I

Jesus is condemned to death

Pilate washes his hands in front of the crowd.

'I am innocent of this man's blood.'

Then he hands over Jesus to be crucified.

Lord, I am Pilate every time I fail to do what is right or allow injustice to happen or blame others for my failures. For the times I have washed my hands of my responsibilities,

Lord have mercy.

We adore you, O Christ and we bless you, because by your cross you have redeemed the world.

2

Jesus takes up the cross

The hands of Jesus grasp the cross as he takes upon himself my sins and the sins of all the world.

Lord it is for love of me that you take up the cross and place it upon your bruised and bleeding shoulder.

For the times I have burdened others with my selfishness,

Lord, have mercy.

We adore you, O Christ and we bless you, because by your cross you have redeemed the world.

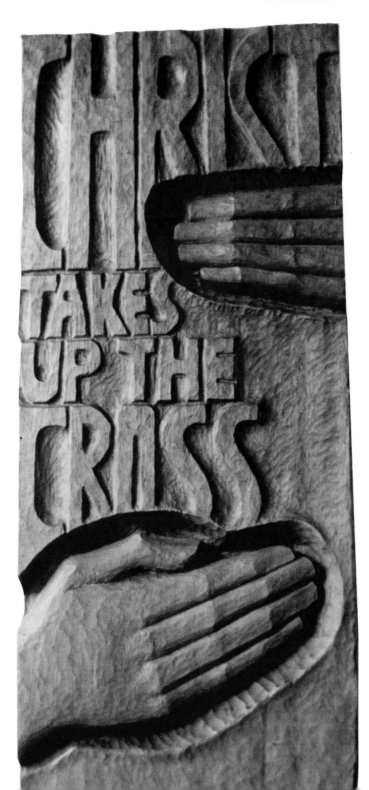

3   Jesus falls for the first time

Jesus' foot slips on the rough
cobbled street and he falls heavily
to the ground, crushed beneath
the weight of the cross.

Lord, my weakness is the cause of
your weakness, my fall is the cause
of your fall. May your rising again
give me strength to rise too from
my falls. For the times I have fallen
or caused others to fall,

Lord have mercy.

We adore you, O Christ and we
bless you, because by your cross
you have redeemed the world.

4 Jesus meets His Mother

Mary, the mother of Jesus,
the mother of sorrows,
meets her son on his journey
and suffers with him for
our salvation.

Lord, by her compassion
your mother took part in
your work of redemption.
May we too share your
agony so that we can
rejoice in your victory.

For the times I have been
indifferent to the sufferings
of others.

Lord have mercy.

We adore you, O Christ
and we bless you, because
by your cross you have
redeemed the world.

5 Simon of Cyrene helps Jesus to carry the cross

The strong hand of Simon takes some
of the burden of the cross and eases
the weight on the shoulders of Jesus.

Lord, you are the creator of heaven
and earth, yet you need the help of
my hands to carry out your work of
mercy in this world. For the times I
have done nothing to ease the burdens
of others,

Lord have mercy.

We adore you, O Christ and we bless
you, because by your cross you have
redeemed the world.

6

Veronica wipes the face of Jesus

The face of Jesus remains imprinted on the towel with which Veronica wiped away his sweat and blood.

Lord, as often as I do an act of kindness to the least of your brothers or sisters, I do it to you. For the times I have failed to see you in the sufferings of others,

Lord have mercy.

We adore you, O Christ and we bless you, because by your cross you have redeemed the world.

7 Jesus falls the second time

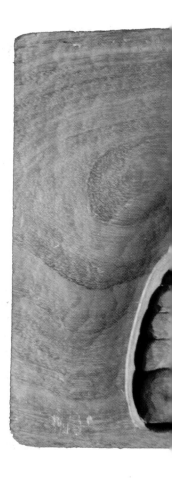

Once again Jesus loses his footing and falls full length upon the hard unyielding street.

Lord, you know that my heart is as hard and unyielding as the street on which you fall.

Help me to weep for your
sufferings and my sins. For
the times I have hardened
my heart against your grace,

Lord have mercy.

We adore you, O Christ and
we bless you, because by
your cross you have
redeemed the world.

8 Jesus meets the women of Jerusalem

The women of Jerusalem weep for Jesus. 'Weep rather for yourselves', he tells them, 'and for your children.'

Lord, we weep for ourselves and for our children. Spare us from the threat of war and destruction that hangs over the world. For all the hatred and cruelty in the world,

Lord have mercy.

We adore you, O Christ and we bless you, because by your cross you have redeemed the world.

9 Jesus falls the third time

The hand of Jesus scarcely has the strength to lift him from the ground, yet he rises again and continues on his way.

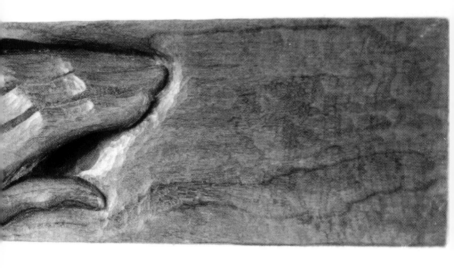

Lord, I am weak and
helpless without you, but
you give me your strength
and I will move mountains.
For the times I have lost
heart and been tempted
to despair,

Lord have mercy.

We adore you, O Christ
and we bless you, because
by your cross you have
redeemed the world.

10

Jesus is stripped of his Garments

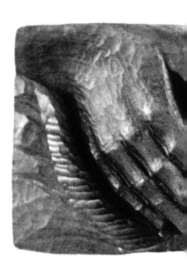

The soldiers strip Jesus of his garments and throw dice for the bloodstained robe he wore on the way to Calvary.

Lord, I am too much in
love with the things of
this world, so worthless in
comparison with the things
of heaven. For the times I
have set my heart on this
world rather than on you,

Lord have mercy.

We adore you, O Christ
and we bless you, because
by your cross you have
redeemed the world.

II

Jesus is nailed to the cross

The nail is hammered
through the flesh of Jesus
with a noise that echoes
throughout the universe.

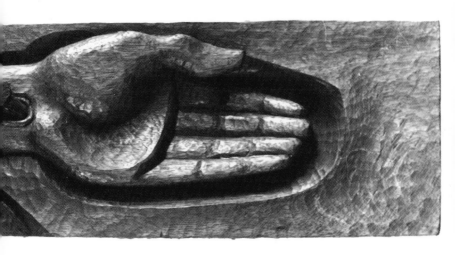

Lord, you suffered willingly
for my sake. Give me
strength when I have to
suffer for your sake. For my
fear of having to suffer in
the cause of right,

Lord have mercy.

We adore you, O Christ
and we bless you, because
by your cross you have
redeemed the world.

12

Jesus dies on the cross

'Father, into your hands I entrust my spirit.' Jesus bows his head and dies.

Lord Jesus Christ, you are my saviour and my king, you are my hope and my refuge, you are my Lord and my God. For my sins and the sins of all the world,

Lord have mercy.

We adore you, O Christ and we bless you, because by your cross you have redeemed the world.

13

Jesus is taken down from the cross

Mary stood by the cross of Jesus when others had deserted him and run away. Now she receives his body into her loving arms.

Lord, on the cross you gave us Mary your mother to be our mother too. May she love and protect us now and at the hour of our death. For the times I have failed in love towards Mary my mother,

Lord have mercy.

We adore you, O Christ and we bless you, because by your cross you have redeemed the world.

14

Jesus is laid in the tomb

At rest in the tomb, Jesus
awaits his resurrection,
when the wounds of pain
will be transformed into
the wounds of glory.

Lord, the ordeal is over,
the victory is won.
Remember me when you
come into your kingdom.

For the times I háve feared
death and forgotten the
resurrection,

Lord have mercy.

We adore you, O Christ
and we bless you, because
by your cross you have
redeemed the world.